SLEEPING LITTLE GIRL, WAKE UP!

A BOOK ON A TRANSFORMATION OF PHARMACEUTICAL BUSINESS EXPERIENCE INTO A BEAUTIFUL LIFE STORY

LARA SOTLAR URANKAR

BALBOA.PRESS

A DIVISION OF HAY HOUSE

Balboa Press books may be ordered through booksellers or by contacting:

Balboa Press
A Division of Hay House
1663 Liberty Drive
Bloomington, IN 47403
www.balboapress.com
844-682-1282

Because of the dynamic nature of the Internet, any web addresses or
links contained in this book may have changed since publication and
may no longer be valid. The views expressed in this work are solely those
of the author and do not necessarily reflect the views of the publisher,
and the publisher hereby disclaims any responsibility for them.

The author of this book does not dispense medical advice or prescribe the use
of any technique as a form of treatment for physical, emotional, or medical
problems without the advice of a physician, either directly or indirectly. The
intent of the author is only to offer information of a general nature to help
you in your quest for emotional and spiritual well-being. In the event you use
any of the information in this book for yourself, which is your constitutional
right, the author and the publisher assume no responsibility for your actions.

Any people depicted in stock imagery provided by Getty Images are
models, and such images are being used for illustrative purposes only.
Certain stock imagery © Getty Images.

Print information available on the last page.

ISBN: 978-1-9822-6936-4 (sc)
ISBN: 978-1-9822-6938-8 (hc)
ISBN: 978-1-9822-6937-1 (e)

Library of Congress Control Number: 2021910489

Balboa Press rev. date: 09/23/2021

There is still time
to become who you've always wanted to be.

Luri and Vaal,
Everything is possible.

CONTENTS

FOREWORD

I sometimes think that, in our society, sales skills are the only thing that counts.

Without mastering marketing techniques, you're lost nowadays—you don't exist.

-or-

You're lost nowadays without mastering marketing techniques; you don't exist. More than anything else, you better get around damn well while selling yourself to an employer amid fierce competition, or while owning your own business. If you don't get around well and don't know how to promote yourself in the market, and if you're not likable personally or visually (according to our society's strict criteria), having a good product or a shining talent seems to matter little. Worst of all, what is being sold, or how it's being sold will no longer matter—as long as it is selling. It does not seem to matter how silly, unnecessary, low quality, or unprofessional it is. What saddens me most is that due to the high expectations of companies, many marketing professionals succumb to one specific goal—selling at all costs. The end justifies the means. Some people are already growing up believing that meeting sales goals and accumulating material goods are the only things that matter in life. Our environment encourages us to keep buying things we don't even need, not considering other people when attempting to reach sales goals. Reaching sales goals is fine—but doing so egotistically and thoughtlessly is not.

And so, I've noticed that many people who have not allowed themselves to be swallowed up by capitalism often feel trapped and inferior. There are individuals and their yearning souls who, on the one hand, only want to create peace according to their principles that are not in line with greedy consumerism. On the other hand, though, there's a system that doesn't allow them to do that. I believe that there are middle paths, or paths that involve connecting and cooperating, that are purer and more evolved that offer man love and, along with it, acceptance and compassion.

So, do we have to push people at all costs for them to buy something from us—or can we be unobtrusive, compassionate salesmen?

Lara Sotlar Urankar, the author of *Sleeping Little Girl, Wake Up!* offers a superb deliberation on this topic. While in an essentially negative mindset about the unstoppable nature of consumerism, I read her book in one sitting. Through her experience, she reminds us that because of the pressure created by capitalism—and the stress that comes with it—we often forget how to find meaning in sales: how to grow personally as a sales agent, and how to respect and love people—instead of egotistically striving to achieve a goal (i.e., highest sales possible).

Her answer is simple. When selling, don't just see yourself and profits. In her own words:

"Change the word 'sell' to the word 'help' and the results will come by themselves."

Each interaction should not just be for "the purpose of buying or selling." These interactions could be a wonderful opportunity to get to know your fellow man, to listen to them, and to try to understand their needs—and worries. . Let the person feel that we carry love and understanding in our hearts and not just yearning for profits.

Lara, whose work deeply satisfies her and who's been successful at marketing medications for an international pharmaceutical company, knows that having such a caring attitude allows results to come by themselves sooner or later. You just have to believe and persist on your path.

Reading Lara's book will provide you with excellent and very concrete advice on how to realize yourself in sales while spreading understanding and respect. It will teach you how to become approachable to strangers (buyers) and how to lend them a helping hand—even if that means you won't earn a dime that day.

We're all part of a consumer society that can be ferocious and unrelenting. However, each individual carries love in their heart. An individual's decision to succumb to the egotistical and self-important rat race—or to put that part of their pure soul into work (which sheer lust for profit cannot infect)—is in each individual's own hands. They may not get rich today, and may never strike it big, but does it really matter? What matters is that they do their best to stay human, regardless of the experience waiting for them. There's no guarantee the path will be easy, yet it is the only path to their inner peace and contentment.

The author of *Sleeping Little Girl, Wake Up!* is a wonderful woman and mother. She has the beauty of inner power needed to fulfill her dreams, with an ear for understanding the needs of herself, the members of her own family, and even the wishes of her employer and colleagues. She does not need to trample other people to achieve her goals. Instead, she works together with others, which is why she can lead any woman who's arrived at a crossroads in her life by the power of her example.

That's why she's also a COOL MOM (which is, by the way, the name of a club of mothers she founded at the school where her children are attending), a "medicine seller" with a big heart, and now, the author of the book *Sleeping Little Girl, Wake Up!* that will be sure to inspire wandering, lost souls.

I've had the opportunity to meet her personally, for which I'm deeply grateful. Marketing is my field of work, too, and I cannot tell you how often I'd felt I was doing something wrong because I hadn't been making profits for my company at all costs. Instead, I've been honest with people rather than solely trying to sell my product to them. I was told I didn't know how to sell. But now, I understand that I'm actually doing a good job. Thank you, Lara, for this.

I persist in finding those paths to achieving small, large, and short and long-term goals that won't hurt others. When I benefit others, I feel that I benefit myself. When I work only for myself and the capital, I'm downright unhappy. It's increasingly apparent to me how honesty, open-mindedness, kind words, and a willingness to help customers after the purchase bring happier, more relaxed, and grateful faces into my life.

Alenka Ivančič, Author of *She, who catches dreams (Lovilka sanj)*

"A child can teach an adult three things:
To be happy for no reason,
To always be busy with something,
And to know how to demand with all his might that
which he desires."

- Paulo Coelho

PREFACE

I felt that something in my life was finally going to shift and change. In a dream, I had seen her. I had heard a bird's song and someone thumbing through a book.

Within a week, I was sitting at her seminar, taking in her practical advice on how to publish a book. *Finally*! I thought to myself. *I've always known I'd be writing books!* And four long years have passed since my first book idea was born.

Two years before, I had gifted a colleague her bestselling book *American Millionaires Have Spoken (Ameriški milijonarji so spregovorili),* and after having done so, pondered about meeting her someday. That was when her life story completely astounded me as well as her youthful spirit and her courage. As I was reading her first book *What We Weren't Taught at School (*Česar *nas niso naučili v* šolah*)*, which she had published in the flush of her youth, I was staggered by the amount of time I needed to experience and realize those very insights myself.

At the seminar, Petra Škarja prompted us to fill out a form and to write down the reason why we would like to publish a book. Usually, she then chooses the individuals she believes in and helps them to publish their books.

I was certain she was going to choose me; after all, I had dreamt of her.

And that's how she became one of the "Greatest Teachers" in my life—as well as a nightmare. The day we first met up, I only had a bit of written content with me, and the rest, I kept in my head. The best thoughts and sentences occur to me when I am alone on the road. The time I spend travelling is the only time I have when I'm completely alone. Late at night, I'm usually not able to sit at the computer and write freely.

Looking back, it now feels like my unfulfilled childhood dream started to unfold with lightning speed as soon as I chose to act in earnest. Without Petra, I probably would have faltered in writing and publishing a book for many years to come. Each week, she asks me how I'm doing and "where I am in the book." However, week in and week out, I continue to feel awkward in front of her

"It's time you got to work," I told myself, and finally started copying my draft onto my computer.

I don't know what the future holds for me, but I sense that what I'm doing now is my mission. Among all the opportunities for experiencing joy, I most look forward to meeting new people and learning from them.

Petra, you certainly are one of these people. Thank you for being.

CHAPTER ONE

THE CHILDREN HAVE THEIR OWN PATH

"If you want to get to know a man,
Observe how he behaves;
If you want to get to know a child,
Observe how he plays."

- Author Unknown

A SLEEPING LITTLE GIRL

The Philippines: Palawan - El Nido

It was early morning when Luri and I were walking across a soft, sandy beach in a small, yet increasingly touristic Filipino village called El Nido.

High hills and resplendent nature were all around us. While the beach was mostly abuzz with life at night, at the moment, people were scarce. The little wooden docked boats that would take masses of tourists to the most beautiful beaches in the world every day were floating lonesomely near the beach. One could only see the locals, who revealed the secrets of the underwater world to tourists during the day, mounted with scuba tanks, returning to their boats to prepare for these excursions.

I felt calm. Calm within and without. Luri and I were alone, watching the crabs coming out of their shells... One could catch sight of them for just a glimpse, then they would sink into the sand again.

This sense of peace was pierced by her question, "Mom, what did you want to be when you were my age?"

"My goodness. What a question at this age!" I replied. Her question hit me right where I struggle most with myself when travelling. Of course an eight-year-old wanted to know her momma's dream. She fell silent, as if wanting to give me some time to think. Her big, brown eyes stared curiously at me, expecting an answer.

The silence was reaching to the furthest depths of my being.

Her words awoke the sleeping little girl within. Once upon a time, I had locked this little girl with such great dreams, expectations, longings, disappointments, and sadness into a drawer and turned the light off.

Life continued its course. Luri helped me to summon this hidden part of me. Hurriedly, I explained to her that her grandfather's greatest wish for me was to become a doctor. I had never fulfilled his expectation because I had become a vet. I loved animals, and so, at the age of 18, I thought it was a good alternative.

During my studies, I had the chance to work with wild animals and dreamed of living among orangutans in the Indonesian rainforest or among African elephants. In reality, however, I had never really wanted to heal only cats, dogs, and cows.

A WRITER

"But, I've always wanted to write; to be a writer," I whispered.

"Yes, I thought so," remarked Luri. "You've got so many books and you read every day."

I remember mentioning to my parents once how much I had wanted to study journalism. My father explained to me at once that I could still write if I really wanted, but that it was better for me to choose some other, more "esteemed" vocation.

The mother of one of Luri's schoolmates confided in us, too: "For a long time, it must have been about ten years, I never shared with anyone that my basic training was as a preschool childcare worker assistant. I thought it was an inferior vocation. Having my own children now, I can see what an important job it is."

The mother of another of Luri's schoolmates said, "I've loved sewing since I was very young. But, since I had been very good at school, my parents thought it was unthinkable to train as a seamstress." Today, she's a proud mother of three daughters, whom she dresses in her exquisite works of art.

"Mom, you can still become a writer, you know. I'll help you. We'll sit together and we'll write a book. You set the book price and I'll sell all the copies. I promise," spoke Luri eagerly and convincingly.

As I'm away on business more often than not, she's convinced that one has to work without stopping to survive, and have at least three jobs. She can't wait to start making her own money. At the age of eight, she already has a detailed plan for a job search. She's written her first job application, and she has every intention of going door to door to ask people if they have work for her; she is a natural businesswoman. I'm sure many unemployed adults rarely have such courage. Many prefer to wait at home and feel sorry for themselves.

Her words moved me deeply. When I gave birth to her and her brother, who is a little older, I forgot about myself. Constantly having to care for two young children and a demanding job left no room for myself.

So one day, I simply discovered I was gone. Somewhere along the way I had not only lost my dream, but also myself.

That's what happens to many women my age, who, due to caring for their families and increasingly demanding jobs, cease to dream and lose their sense of self. One might be unhappy at work, but simply too weary in the evening to think about, let alone to deal with, a problem.

However, somewhere deep within, there still lives a sleeping little girl who needs to be awakened.

A SINGER AND A TENNIS PLAYER

"You know, I'll be a singer," said Luri decisively. "I've already started. Vaal could not believe I was really going to sing the *Little Terrace* song on the plane. But I sang it," she proudly explained.

How proud I was of her when, during the flight from the Philippine island of Cebu to Palawan, the flight attendant invited her to sing into the microphone, and she fearlessly sang a beautiful Slovenian song.

"Vaal wouldn't have had the courage," she spontaneously remarked.

Vaal is eleven and wants to become a top professional tennis player. Since he was five, he has believed he would one day win the tournament at Wimbledon. When I share this with my acquaintances, they usually respond by saying, "Nonsense. It's impossible anyway. Do you even know how few really make it? How many give up? Do you know what kind of results he would have to score today in order to succeed someday? No chance. You're wasting your time and money."

Today, these words no longer dampen me. Who am I to shatter my child's dream? I want him to believe in his dream, and I want him to believe that anything is possible. My duty is to encourage him and to ensure his healthy physical and mental development. Interestingly, he's been saving pocket money for a few years for books on sportsmen, in spite of "not really having a great interest in reading." On his bedside table there are biographies of Nadal, Đoković, Federer, and many other tennis greats.

How their stories move him! He learns something from all of them. Following Đoković's example, he always carries a banana in his sports bag, believes in performing rituals prior to a match, and he's especially proud that his mom works in a pharmaceutical company, just like Federer's father once did.

Vaal's tennis coach once said that Vaal was like a diamond that only needed to be cut out. To this, I would add that all he lacks to live a successful life is courage. As opposed to Luri, who has early on in her life enjoyed the company of young and spontaneous teachers that allow children to freely explore the world, Vaal had a teacher who never professed the importance of courage.

THE MIRROR

One day, I was sitting in a hall full of parents at a Waldorf school my children attend, where the headmaster had organized a round table discussion with Ivo Boscarol—CEO of Pipistrel, a producer of ultralight and light aircraft, based in Slovenia. Boscarol is most known as an aircraft designer and entrepreneur—and I was deep in thought.

Listening to his life story, I was thrilled by his life philosophy.

From his speech, one could feel that he loves his work, basks in it, and that he believes in himself and his employees. He knows the best ideas are born where working environments are at ease. It felt good to hear that his employees can confide in him whenever their focus wanders or whenever they feel they aren't able to live up to their potential. We all have days of smooth sailing at work—and days when the waters get rough. This is human. And that's when Ivo Boscarol's employees are given the chance to either stay at home or stay at work and play pool or other games together.

That's when something within began to say, "How can you tell your children every day that they can succeed in whatever they choose... that Luri can sing on the grandest stages in the world and Vaal can be not only a spectator but a tennis player at Wimbledon?

"How are they going to believe that their dreams are achievable if you have forgotten your own dream from so long ago? What have you done yourself? Have you been living your own life the way you dreamed of doing? What are your plans—not for your children, but for YOU? What are YOU going to be doing in a month, in two months, in half a year or in two years?"

When Vaal used to train for soccer, I could hardly wait until he tired of it. Why? Time and again, I would witness parents throwing tantrums.

The children were five and six years old, and their parents expected them to play soccer like professionals. They'd shout at their children, and even slap them now and then. "How can you be so slow? How did you not see the goal was empty? Why did you pass the ball? Why didn't you kick the ball into the goal?" They could be heard reproaching their children. There are many more similar examples.

What does a shouting father or a mother who suddenly has turned into a soccer expert do to help their child be successful at soccer? The father probably does nothing, and the same is probably true for the mother. They are both chasing rainbows in their own sports illusion. All too often, parents stick their noses into the work of coaches. The mother of Peter Prevc, a Slovenian ski jumping champion, once said that she trusted her sons to their coaches because they knew what they were doing. When Vaal asks me about tennis, I usually answer, "Ask Tjaša (his coach), she knows the strategies in tennis. Follow the way she teaches you."

When he competes at a tournament, I see him off with the words, "Do not fear those that are better than you. Be grateful to be playing with them. That's how you'll learn something from them and have quality training. Make sure you have fun while playing. In any case, everyone is beatable, even the best. Just do your best." What I really want him to do is to maintain his joy.

So, in this day and age, one can see that the value of trust has largely been lost.

The same holds true with school and grades. Since I was burdened with achieving good grades all my life, as grades meant a great deal to my parents, I'm overjoyed with the fact that I can offer my children a life with no grades. They attend Waldorf School, where there is no numerical grading in the early years.

Their childhood is nothing like mine was. When they come home from school, I never first ask them about the grades they got. I always ask what they have learned.

I keep hearing complaints from my friends, whose children are overloaded with grades, and who are being done an injustice by having the joy of painting, sports, music, and many other things taken from them. Moms compete by comparing whose child is getting the better grades, being more praised, entering more competitions, and attending more extracurricular activities, as that is how their sense of worth seemingly grows, too.

In her admirable musings, Psychologist Dr. Metka Mencin Ceplak says, "A much greater problem than the weight of schoolbags and the number of hours studying is that success defines a child's 'worth', and that it also determines 'the worthiness' of their parents."

Just yesterday, Vaal brought home some wisdom from his class teacher. Since they've been learning about Ancient Greece and the theorems of Socrates, the class teacher added some wisdom of his own, which took Vaal by surprise and left him pondering for some time.

The teacher told them, "Your grades are not the measure of your success in life. Some of the students with the lowest grades have become the world's top sportsmen, artists, and inventors."

I'm happy I don't have any expectations whatsoever about what my children will be. My only wish for them is to love with all their heart what they choose to do.

TIME

Is this my midlife crisis already? I've crossed the magic age limit of forty and am convinced that I've missed the right time for everything.

Despite having achieved a great deal over the years, travelled across a large part of the world, created a beautiful family, and, as my best friend Damjan says, managed to be counted among the small percentage of the world's population which has a high enough living standard that I don't have to worry about the price of basic living necessities, I knew deep down that I wasn't living the life I wanted.

And it wasn't about my income.

It was about my life's purpose. My free will. My free time. As a result of my perpetual hurrying, overworking, and chronic fatigue, I had let go of my dreams. I had lived from day to day, from one obligation to another.

My only so-called "breather" is our annual holiday. I knew that if I organized our trip at least a few months ahead, I could survive all the strain that awaited until the holiday. Travelling has long been my way of escaping from reality, or, from another point of view, it has meant living life to the fullest. To me, it is a complete breather. Travelling with two little children has never been exhausting to me, as long as I can go and recharge. They're now growing up, and I wonder, *Do I really have to wait all year long and work hard each day in order to spend a few weeks with my children on holiday, which is the only time when I am really me?*

A friend of mine was astonished by us when our families first travelled together. Our children are the same age and are best friends.

Back when we were both pregnant, we spoke of being in love

with Africa and how we would take our children to the African wilderness, where they would see elephants and lions, and breathe the air that I am so addicted to. When our girls finally turned five, we all travelled to Tanzania. Both her and her husband couldn't believe how different I really was; how calm and relaxed I could be when I'm in harmony with myself.

Do you know what your goal is? In a month, in half a year …? Where do you see yourself in a year, in five years? I can safely assert that most people don't know the answer to these questions.

One day at work, we were honored to meet and listen to a lecture held by one of the greatest Slovenian sportswomen, Petra Majdič, a cross-country skier. In her career, Petra had achieved everything she had set out to accomplish. All of Slovenia breathed with her when, in 2010 at the Vancouver Olympic Games, she came in third place. She became a Slovenian national heroine, a symbol of perseverance and stamina.

These qualities were on display when, during the race, which she had been training for many years, she fell into the gutter beside the track and broke her ribs. But she had a clear goal—a medal. She clenched her teeth and, by drawing on the last reservoir of her strength, won that which had been her goal for years. She had a vision.

Petra Majdič asked us during her speech what our personal (not professional) goal was and when we were going to accomplish it

"No idea," I sighed. I've been meaning to write a book for years; there are at least three different books I have wanted to write, and still I've done absolutely nothing yet. I still leave for work early in the morning and work all day. I hardly find time for myself, and when my friends ask me if I'm thinking about my future—as if to say that things cannot go on like this indefinitely—I reply that I'm trying to set things right.

FEAR

Of course, first comes the thought: an idea is never born without simultaneously activating the power to realize it.

Then there's the word: whatever you say and promise to do, needs to be done. Suddenly, I started announcing to everyone that I was writing a book. Before I wrote it, I had already started negotiating the sales. My husband observed me and asked worriedly, "Are you sure you're going to finish the book by then?"

Of course I was sure. Negotiating for the book sale pushed me to do what I had promised to do.

And here are my actions. They say it all.

My firm belief is that the most powerful weapon which pushes me to prove to my children—by the power of my example—is that anything in life is possible.

I know that it isn't too late, and I know what I want. I know which path to take to arrive at where I want to be. My environment supports me. I know how I want to live. But just before taking a big step, FEAR stops me.

Fear? Have we met and finally looked into each other's eyes?

I needed a long time to discover what it was that kept me from what I wanted. And one day I understood that, too.

When you're writing a book, you open up your heart, so the readers can see who you really are. The light in which I will shine, when I fully become who I am, will be seen far and wide. And that's what I was afraid of; to be seen and of others' envy of me.

Because I love my children, I've turned fear away, so that I could step out of my comfort zone, the safety net I had been wrapped up in for so many years.

Working at an international company has made me strong and experienced, so that I feel ready to face all that shining brightness brought on by the light.

Ask yourself, "What is it that keeps me from fulfilling my dream?" If you face your fear, you'll turn it away, and your path will open up. It will then be easy to follow.

BE THE CHANGE YOU WISH TO SEE

We often blame others for our own misery and dissatisfaction. It's difficult to admit that it's not anybody else's fault. It's all up to us how we are going to view and accept a situation.

Change is the only constant in life and one has to accept it with open arms, because change brings the new experiences that we have to have on our path through life.

If you're keen on soccer, don't force your son to become the "next Messi." I'm not saying it isn't too late to become a top professional soccer player—but you can become a top amateur.

It's never too late.

When I was a teenager, I started reading spiritual self-help books. I read many, and one day, my mom told me, "You know, to live a happy life, it is enough to remember a single sentence from each book you read."

A single sentence is enough to change your world.

But only if you are willing to see the world differently!

I'm offering you my own box of medicine called COURAGE.

When you feel you've lost your path, there's a magic pill available to you, which drives away all dark, negative thoughts and shows the way:

**Don't pass the burden of your unfulfilled
desires onto your children.
Even if it is late (better late than never), realize your
dream and help your children fulfil theirs.**

CHAPTER TWO

DO WHAT YOU LOVE

WORKING AT AN INTERNATIONAL
PHARMACEUTICAL COMPANY
What have I learned and how can I use this
knowledge in my job or in my daily life?

*"Cherish your vision and your dreams, as they
are the children of your soul, the blueprints of your
ultimate achievements."*

- Napoleon Hill

WEAPONS, DRUGS, AND MEDICINE

"If you cannot convince them, confuse them."
- Harry S. Truman

We spend most of our time at work—one third of our day, to be exact. I believe some people spend even more time at work. Our work inadvertently affects everything that is going on in our personal life, and it is significant for our personal growth. More often than not, our children are victims of their parents' bad moods, which stem from the parents' dissatisfaction and work overload.

The work environment, with its various challenges and interactions with people, gives us the opportunity to get to know who we really are. This allows us to cultivate our skills, which we can then put to good advantage outside the work environment.

For this reason, I want to write about what I know very well— and most people don't—yet, in spite of not knowing this well, they often condemn it. People love to judge things without learning about them. I repeatedly read and hear comments on how the pharmaceutical industry wishes ill upon people, is only interested in making profits, that we are on the dark side, etc. What I wish is to break these beliefs that people who don't even know what we do, have about our work. I also wish to share how working at an international pharmaceutical company can shape a person.

There is a general belief out there that weapons, drugs, and pharmaceuticals control the world. Whenever there's a new pandemic and the sudden panic that comes with it starts sweeping the world, people are always sure the pharmaceutical industry is behind it; this industry that is driven by an insatiable thirst for profits.

"You're making money again," people prod me, when the media covers an ebola or zika outbreak, or some other imminent disease. Such provocations don't get to me anymore.

When we met by chance in front of our building recently, an acquaintance of mine told me, "You work in pharmacy and know exactly what's going to befall us." The same person then thought about it for a few days and came to me with a new proposal, "There's a lot of money in pharmacy. I'd like to work at your company, too."

One rarely admits to bringing disease upon oneself mostly by oneself. We know not what we drink, eat, and breathe. And then stress and hurry are added. I'm one of those people who knows exactly what is bad for my health, yet I do not take even half an hour a day to do something for myself. When I come home from work, I'm occupied with my children's school and after-school activities, I cook and tidy—in other words, I serve my family. And I continue to hope that I'll start changing things before an illness befalls me.

Days, months, and years fly by. I still haven't done anything.

How many of you are aware of people working at pharmaceutical companies with the purpose of helping others—not just imposing medicines on doctors, as people often believe we do?

Pharmaceutical companies in Slovenia:

- Invest in the research and development of new medicines;
- Produce medicines and offer new jobs every year;
- Employ the young, the elderly, and less and more educated people and help them grow;
- Do clinical research and thus offer patients access to medicines before they are offered on the market;
- Ensure an undisturbed supply of medicines to the market;

- Make people aware of illnesses through financial support and various projects, so that illnesses are recognized in time;
- Enable a higher quality of life;
- Treat and heal people indirectly;
- Extend people's life span;
- Issue publications for the lay public;
- Offer financial support to patient associations;
- Offer financial support for the education of health workers;
- Support and help Slovenian experts to cooperate abroad;
- Donate for the purchase of medical equipment, appliances, etc.;
- Bring foreign experts to Slovenia;
- Cooperate with local communities and strive to benefit society; and
- Slovenia collects the highest number of taxes from successful pharmaceutical companies.

And the list goes on and on.

Do you do this kind of work, too? Are you part of the pharmaceutical industry?

Then you should be really proud of yourself!

And to all of you who look daggers at representatives of pharmaceutical companies as they make their way through waiting rooms: think about it, perhaps one day the information in their black briefcases will help you live a better life, too.

The idea for this book was born when, after a full-day course on business ethics, I spoke with my colleagues about the kind of knowledge we had all acquired while working in pharmacy. We were brimming with ideas about where and how we could use our skills. One of my colleagues thought managing a prison would be a good challenge for him, another colleague thought organizing work in public administration by focusing on tasks and setting goals would be great, and the third colleague wanted to reintroduce work brigades.

And on the other side—there are women my age, mothers who rush all days and serve. To their employer, to their children, to their parents, to others. But to themselves, to all these mothers, I wish to lay this on their hearts:

Your children only have one mother. You are invaluable. Stop, and first take care of yourself.

This is how this book came to be, and I hope it can be:

- A compass to all mothers, who have lost themselves in their daily responsibilities and only need a pinch of courage to awaken the sleeping little girl within;
- Encouragement for all parents to raise their children by the power of their own example and not by demanding something from them;
- Inspiration to all people to begin to fulfil their purpose and not be afraid to let their light shine;
- A push to all who've long tried to change something but don't do anything;
- A textbook to all who are starting their path in the pharmaceutical industry and wonder from time to time what in the world they are doing;
- An enlightenment to all who've persisted in pharmacy for many years but aren't aware of how important their work is and how many people they've indirectly helped to heal,

improve their quality of life or extend their life. And no one has ever told them THANK YOU;

- Hope to all patients and their relatives that there are people out there who are striving to find new medicines and enable access to these new medicines;
- Acknowledgment to all my "Great Teachers," who helped me become the person I am today; and
- Proof that it's never too late.

If I could do it, you can do it!

Before passing judgement,
Look around yourself,
And look at yourself, too.
Then dare to judge.

YOU ARE NOW WHERE YOU NEED TO BE

*"There is a single way to feel good; we need to learn
to be happy with what is given to us, and not always
demand what we are currently lacking."*

- Theodor Fontane

I had a job that I liked. I liked my colleagues, and although
I would leave home early to take the train at 5 a.m. and come
back only in the evening, it wasn't too hard for me. It was my
first job and I was young and determined. But I was working at
a public institution, doing official tasks, and in spite of having
graduated from a veterinary faculty, my salary was low, with no
chance of promotion in the following five years. My scope of work
was protecting animals against cruelty. Slovenia had to harmonize
its legislation with that of the European Union as we were about to
become an EU country. My salary was so low I couldn't even afford
to live an independent life. I had just gotten married and someday
wanted to have children. But how could I have made it possible for
them to have all that I believed children need? How could I afford
quality diapers, let alone a kindergarten education, and all the costs
that come with the birth of a child? My greatest passion was to travel,
but with my salary at the time I couldn't buy even an air ticket (at
this point in time there were no low-cost airlines).

After having graduated, my best friend and faculty classmate,
Damjan, got his first job at a representative office of a foreign
pharmaceutical company. He got a new company car, an excellent
salary, and often went on business trips. Two years had passed, and
he was looking at the weary me and wondering why I was working

for such a low salary. When their company was looking for new colleagues, he advised me to go for a job interview. I had no idea what to do as I loved my job, but I wanted to have children.

So I gathered my courage and went for the job interview. After waiting for the company manager for a few hours, I finally had my interview. It went smoothly—I made it plain and simple that I wanted to have a child in the near future, and that I wasn't willing to give up having a child because of a new job. When she assured me that that wasn't a problem and asked me if I agreed with the proposed salary, she left me speechless. Now what? Her offer seemed to be more than just tempting. The sum she offered to me exceeded the salary I had been receiving by several times.

I liked the manager. There really was no need to think much about the offer, and all I was supposed to do, as Damjan had explained to me, was to visit clients, mainly doctors and pharmacists, and present them the newest medical research results involving our medicines.

I accepted the job and couldn't even imagine the significance of the step I had just taken in my life. I had no idea that a job like that existed, let alone that the job would be what I had dreamed about. I had dreamed about working with wild animals, so I studied veterinary medicine, acquired additional education in the United States and in Africa, and worked at one of the best zoos in the world. Pharmacy, medicine, and medications? I was done with that when I had never signed up to study medicine.

How many times was I angry and disappointed with myself for choosing pharmacy over all the other jobs in this world.

I intended to work there for two years, yet I have now spent fifteen years at the same pharmaceutical company.

Today, I'm infinitely grateful for having such a huge opportunity for personal growth.

When I quit my first job, the manager disappointedly stated, "You've sold yourself for money." Not only for money. For an infinite number of experiences, and for growth. During all these years, I've met so many new people, seen so many new places, and learned diligently.

Working at a public institution is nice, as an individual can secure a safe, relatively calm and stable environment; there's no constant adjusting, and people can stay in their comfort zone until retirement.

When I told my parents I was going to quit my job, they could not believe what I was doing. They thought I had the best, most secure job in the world, where I could wait to see my retirement. But the times have changed and I do not have the same mindset as their generation.

With all the known and proven methods of work, people working in public institutions should, in my opinion, be allowed to make personal progress, and encouraged to make positive change with their ideas, or pushed out of their comfort zones into environments where they can be creative.

People who make such changes usually aren't desirable or people don't like them. Most people prefer to stay in their unchangeable comfort zone; and although they are dissatisfied, they feel safe. No one likes change, as it has never been presented as positive.

When the storm is over and we look back, we can see that the person who removed our safety net did more for us than the one who let us be.

A colleague of mine recently told me, "In my previous job, I had a wonderful boss. She never bugged me, she let me be. Of course, I liked that very much, but I can now see that the comfort she'd given me was precisely why I learned nothing new."

Would you be where you are now if someone had not soured your life from time to time?

Frankly speaking, it took me a long time to reconcile the fact that, among all the available jobs, I was selling medications. It was difficult to ignore people glaring at me in packed waiting rooms, and the nurses tired of the daily crowds and of difficult patients receiving me reluctantly: "Yet another representative." There were days when I cried, wondering, *Why?*

It wasn't until years later that I understood the words of our former managing director. He never really had a way with words, and was never diplomatic. He was blunt and we were all somewhat afraid of him. But he was just. After my first year and a half of working at a new job position, when I felt mentally and physically drained, and he could see for himself how hard I was trying to do my job, he hugged me upon his departure and told me, "Enjoy!"

He must have been the first to notice that in my great desire to prove myself and achieve my goals, I wasn't enjoying my work.

I'm infinitely grateful to him for steering me in the right direction with a single word.

We have to understand that if we want to live our life to the fullest and have no regrets about the things we haven't managed to do, it only takes COURAGE and zero doubts!

We have to TRUST in ourselves.

And so there came the day when I told myself out loud "You have to be here now in order to learn something. Reconcile this within yourself. Accept it. When you have mastered this, you will set yourself free and fly towards your goal."

How many of you do what you've always wanted to do? I know many people who dislike their job. They don't like their job, their superiors, they are bothered by their colleagues, clients, and their work environment. They complain a lot. And I know many sleeping little girls and boys, waiting to be awoken. Few, however, have the courage to wake up.

There are always more options available.

If you intend to keep doing the job you're doing, I recommend you to change the way you perceive it. Stop grumbling, and find in it those things that cause you to feel joy. Find your passion.

That's what I did. I started trusting myself, and I found meaning in what I do; I became aware of the lessons I was experiencing as something that helped me to learn and I began to appreciate all the people who helped me in the process.

Today, my work is my joy. I can be creative, I feel free, and I love both my colleagues and my clients. That's why I persist.

And then success comes by itself.

If you cannot do all that, LEAVE. Find another job.

You are now here in order to learn something.
Resign yourself to it and accept it.
When you have mastered that, you will set
yourself free and fly towards your goal.
It's never too late.

THE HEALTH SELLER

"Do what you can, with what you have, where you are."

- *Thomas Roosevelt*

What do I do? Many people, even my relatives, still don't know what exactly it is. Why do I work so much? Why am I always so tired? Driving to work and back every day, encountering roadblocks every day surely can't be the reason. I've toughened. I spend some time in the office, move around a little bit, and talk about our medications. How simple.

One evening my mother called me on the phone and said, "There's a movie about your job on TV. You should watch it!" I turned on the TV, spread the news about the movie to some of my colleagues, and watched it. It was *The Medicine Seller*, a movie by the Italian movie director Antonio Morabito. Did I find myself in it? Perhaps.

What the protagonist and I had in common was our education—he was a vet, too. The movie is actually very sad and shows the negative side of working at a pharmaceutical company.

My mother called me no earlier than the next evening. She was appalled, "You do all that? I now understand why you are weary and grumpy."

I explained to her that it wasn't so bad, and that I didn't do all of the things that were shown in the movie. "Mom, you know how I am and how you've raised me," I told her, and clarified that some of the acts in the movie went against our industry's ethical values. I, unlike the movie's protagonist, have to be ethical as it's vital for my company that the employees abide strictly by all the rules.

ALL ALONE INTO THE WORLD

"Life isn't about waiting for the storm to pass. It's about learning to dance in the rain."

- Author Unknown

Smile, kindly say hello, and not only will the door open to you but hearts will open, too.

It was five in the morning on March 8th, International Woman's Day. I stood in front of the mirror, tried to conceal the bags under my eyes... and sighed. I tried not to burst in tears. How I was so tired!

After maternity leave, I returned to work, all while still breast-feeding Luri. She had been crying all night and waking up Vaal. She must have felt my restlessness. It was snowing outside and I had to get going. The road to the hospital was winding and full of holes. At 7 a.m., I was scheduled to present new research at a morning doctors' meeting. I was facing a medical room and thirty grim faces. Here and there, a doctor gave me an encouraging smile. *She's a mother, too, and she knows what young women go through every day,* I thought. *What did women fight for decades ago? Was the work they did not enough for them? Why did they want more?* I wondered then. A cold greeting, dead silence, and I was standing before them. Looks, judgment, silence. A question or two.

I was well prepared but I was feeling heartache. I don't know how many of the people who sat there understood that I was only a human being, too; it wasn't easy for me, and that they looked more like cold-hearted inspectors looking for signs of insufficient knowledge within a field they worked in every day. Their self-satisfaction with their knowledge showed that they believed they were worth more than you, and for them you were "yet another person from the pharmacy" wasting their time. They know it all already anyway.

How would they do if they were in my shoes? Would they stay so confident, or would their voices tremble during the lecture?

I took a deep breath and smiled. I showed my confidence and answered their questions.

Looking at them, I thought, *It's not easy for them either. They might have been on duty all night, seen a patient die, or have family problems. They might just feel sleepy, like me.*

At first, I was scared of not being able to answer doctors' questions. Now I know I cannot know it all.

So, if you don't know the answer to a question, always reply calmly, "I don't know the answer. I will find out and will be happy to let you know."

Keep your promise, as this is how you'll gain their trust. No one knows everything. However, you can prepare well in advance for such meetings, and do the best you can.

There's nothing wrong if you hold a piece of paper in your hand and take a peek at it sometimes. It's impossible to know all the numbers by heart. Smart people write and read.

And a smile saves many troubles.

I CAN — I CAN'T? I'D RATHER JUST RUN AWAY

"Never pay any attention to what critics say. A statue has never been set up in honor of a critic."

- Jean Sibelius

When we got a new Great Teacher, she impressed us all at the first presentation she held in front of all the employees.

First and foremost, her presentation was different and a lot of fun. She oozed energy, and since she became my main Great Teacher, I had the chance to learn from the best.

"You think I'm not scared?" she asked me once. "I am. But I always imagine that people listening to me go to the loo just like I do. And to be more at ease, I imagine them without their undies. You know, they are just people."

When preparing a presentation of any sort, it always pays off to take a risk. The listeners are thrilled with anything new and interesting. For me, each and every presentation has to have its story—a common thread. I like to include things that pique the listeners' interest. Let your imagination run free. Show your fun side, warmth, but also your expertise.

All these years, I've had the chance to attend and enjoy many lectures given by leading experts in the field of medicine. Excellent lecturers differ from average ones in their originality.

Preparing lectures is my passion. I love preparing presentations.

It was while practising how to give a lecture correctly that I first realized I was skilled at it. To practice giving a lecture, we were asked to prepare a lecture on something from our daily life—we listened to a lecture on miniature rabbits and floating staircases. Since I had just enrolled Vaal in the first grade of Waldorf School, I presented the manner of teaching at such schools. The proof of my cogency are the children of two colleagues (they didn't have children back then), who are now attending at Waldorf School.

Prepare for your performance. Speak clearly and time yourself. People will notice right away that you've prepared the lecture well, and these will be plus points for you.

When I gave my first presentation to foreigners in a foreign language, I thought I couldn't do it. Is this my end? I could hardly breathe. But my Great Teacher whispered to me at a very opportune moment, "You know so much about this."

I survived and gave an excellent performance.

But the day had merely started after the morning meeting, and there were many more visits to come.

Man can take much more than he thinks he can.

A BLACK BRIEFCASE PAYING A VISIT

*Presents, money, documents? What in the world
is in the briefcase?*

When I began doing fieldwork and visiting several clients a day
(my clients were doctors and pharmacists), the hardest part was to
walk through a waiting room packed with patients.

I knew that some of them had been waiting to see their doctors
for hours. Even though I, too, had set an appointment with a doctor,
I felt uncomfortable with knocking on a nurse's door and asking
if I could see the doctor. If I had asked to see the doctor for only
a minute, I would have been lying, as it took longer, even when a
doctor said they could see me only for a minute. An informal golden
rule and a ticket for the next time is to say you'll be short, then stick
to it.

Due to time constraints and doctors constantly being
overworked, you never know whether you'll succeed in doing your
job as you should. I have seen patients looking daggers at me, and
the questioning, doubting look of a nurse who would have to calm
raging patients, and who never even dreamt of how her words cut
into my heart, "Another rep has arrived."

"What rep?" I wanted to say out loud, but I dared not of course,
because I knew that next time around she would probably turn me
away.

She stared into my briefcase, and if I didn't open it and take out
a pen, she would shamelessly ask me, "Carrying no pen and crib
notes?" The fact that I was carrying no pen and crib notes was largely
due to the nature of the pharmacy industry. There are no more pens

nor post-its nor medicines. There are also fewer and fewer paper documents. In most cases, we're accompanied by tablet computers.

Please, don't misunderstand me. I admire the work of medical nurses and administrators. Despite a huge load of work, most are smiling and kind. Often, it is them who help us most and make our job easier.

I remember entering a waiting room in fear once after a colleague who had been there before told me how, before even knocking on the door, a patient had physically attacked him with an umbrella there. Well, no such thing has happened to me; I've only overheard a number of remarks related to my being there.

It was when I no longer perceived full waiting rooms that I understood that I had made progress at work. It was when I was no longer troubled by when and how to knock on the door and jump over the queue. On my way to the doctor's office, I no longer noticed the hurdles. I was just performing my duty.

Whenever you need to go to a waiting room full of sick and impatient people, I recommend putting on a kind face, smiling, and wishing everyone a loud "Good day." Know you're only conscientiously performing your duty, and if need be, explain that to people.

Don't carry your work briefcase with you as it reveals from afar that you're just another "rep," who is pushing your way into the queue. Instead, decide on a casual, inconspicuous bag, yet one that is big enough for all your work accessories.

What to wear? How do rigid male suits, ties, black bags, vertiginous heels, garishly red nail polish, or excessive make-up make you feel?

My experience is that people will accept you better when you don't stand out. There's nothing wrong with not wearing a tie, and low heels with women are acceptable—especially if you're out in the field all day. Let your most beautiful accessory be your SMILE.

When you first arrive in a doctor's office, what's most important is to introduce yourself to a medical nurse or administrator, say what you do, and that you're looking forward to your joint cooperation. When you express how important and meaningful their work is, you can be sure they will do their best to help you when you need them. You'd be surprised to see how many professional colleagues ignore the most important person at the doctor's side. Have a kind small talk with that person; your work will be easy and it will feel completely different.

To you, our dear helpers—medical nurses and administrators, let me say, you don't know how immensely grateful we are for your warm reception and kind words. Thank you.

If you have a chance, I highly recommend you to set your next appointment in person, at the end of your visit—not over the phone.

And you, dear patients, ask yourselves, if it isn't this very "intruder," whom you scowl at, the very solution to your health problems.

Don't rush to blame, and don't blame unjustly.

THE SECRET IS IN BEING WELL-PREPARED

"To be prepared is half the victory."
- Miguel Cervantes

A vital part of our work is to prepare for a visit. Think well about what it is you'd like to achieve during a visit. Make notes about what you had promised to a doctor last time, and keep your promise. You have to understand that doctors' personalities differ, so you should approach each one of them differently. Adjust to them, but remain who you are. Sometimes it's allowed and sometimes it's forbidden, but it's very useful to make notes on what you had talked about after a meeting. Don't write down everything, only the crucial things. Reading these notes will help you a great deal before your next meeting. It'll take up some of your time, but you'll feel more confident upon arriving at the doctor's office.

And your knowledge? It's important to always be learning. Follow innovations, read studies. Your foundation is your knowledge about a disease and its medicine!

Whenever you go for a meeting, you'll make a better impression if the people you talk to see that you have prepared in advance. It's good to write down some key points that you want to discuss, as well as all the things you've agreed on.

Be confident, since you may know the essentials much better than the person you're talking to.

Learn, learn, learn.

DO I KNOW THE PERSON I'M TALKING TO?

"He who wears a smile instead of worrying is always the strongest."

- Japanese saying

A strong handshake, an easy look in the eyes, and a smile are still our most powerful weapons.

The understanding I got when, after ten years, I revisited a family doctor's office and saw that everything had stayed the same—the staff, the furniture, and the crowd—shifted something in me.

You have to know that doctors are constantly listening to other people talking only about problems. Doctors' heads are full of other people's problems, and so some of the doctors are more than happy to receive a sales representative.

"Finally, I won't be hearing about problems," they like to say, and drop much of that day's burden. There were visits during which I only listened, nodded, agreed, and said absolutely nothing. I felt it was time to be silent and talk about the medicine next time. How could I have discussed medical research with a doctor whose husband left her the day before, and who cried all through the night because her world had fallen apart, and was barely able to hold in the tears? Should I not be a shoulder to cry on to a doctor who had told a young mother that day that she only had a few months to live?

One has to know the proper time to fall silent, the proper time to listen, and the proper time to speak. It may feel like nothing has been accomplished, but perhaps a relationship will be established that will last for many years to come.

Be brief and concise in the meetings. Never overlook a signal that shows the doctor has heard enough.

After they've left university and begun working in the pharmaceutical industry, young people usually don't yet have a sense of when to listen, when to speak, when to wind up, and when to leave. They aren't able to recognize the signal that they've done their job and accomplished their goal. Often, they're working under the direction of countless hours of training on what they should do and how they're supposed to do something so that a medicine gets sold, and thus, they attempt to prove themselves. Usually, they aren't told how to build relationships and trust, and where the limits are. One can only learn that through experience, or never learn it at all.

There are many people I know, who, after many years of fieldwork still have not learned this crucial lesson. The only thing they see is numbers, plans, money, and themselves, but they don't see people. They haven't managed to learn that throughout all these years. They keep banging their heads against brick walls, and wonder why doctors still haven't accepted them, or why sales aren't as good as they should be. The answer is simple: they continue to see themselves only; they don't have patients' interests at heart and don't recognize that doctors are people, too.

One more thing, they only wish to SELL and don't keep in mind the magic word: HELP.

A colleague of mine and I once visited a family doctor in a small town. When she saw us, she was delighted to share how, "If a patient who's being treated with your company's medicine met you now, he would hug and kiss you. You've saved his life! After having received information on this medicine from you, I referred him for further treatment. He found himself in distress and didn't see a way out.

His wife had left him, and he was going to take his own life. The medicine has completely changed his life, and he's living healthily again."

These words completely changed the way I view our work. Whether people talk kindly about us or not, it doesn't matter. Each night, I fall asleep with a clear conscience and with the feeling that my visits to the doctors' offices help many patients heal. I help my fellow men become well again. What is more precious than that?

Change the word "sell" to the word "help" and the results will come by themselves.

Who am I competing with and what are they like?

I stick to the rule to never ever speak ill about my competition. When someone challenges me, I simply prove my facts.

There are hardly any bad medicines in this day and age.

It's people who cause separation.

Don't do to others what you don't want others to do to you.

GET SOME FRESH AIR AND TAKE A BREATH

"All our knowledge has its origins in our perceptions."
- Leonardo da Vinci

After having paid a visit, it's vital to consider what you spoke about, what you might have forgotten, what you could have done differently, and what you accomplished. Plan your next visit. Most of the people never do this, but I guarantee it will make your next meeting incredibly smooth.

Properly organizing your work is crucial to a job well done.

One has to learn when to go all the way, and when to stop where necessary.

Why haven't I changed my job yet? It must be the fact that I didn't know half of my colleagues when I returned to work after my maternity leave (twice). So many faces had changed in a year, and when I was back, a new teacher, new colleagues, new medicines, new clients, and a new part of Slovenia would always be there for me.

And so, I found myself at the beginning yet again. I would have to prove myself over and over again, as my old successes drifted off along with people.

That said, I was able to build good relationships time and again, to learn a new chapter of medicine, to study new medicines, and to discover new places in my homeland using maps (I didn't have GPS back then). Whenever the road takes me to a new place, I still check where a church is, as there's usually a pharmacy standing right next to it, as well as a doctor's office.

Much depends on us and us alone: how we organize our time, how we distribute our work, and how we learn.

Organizing your work well gives you more free time.

WHY ISN'T EVERYONE SUCCESSFUL?

"Many of life's failures are people who did not realize how close they were to success when they gave up."

- *Thomas Edison*

All who know me know that I never bargain.

Instead, I prefer to pay more for something than to ask for a discount. My husband, however, excels at bargaining. To me personally, money doesn't mean much. This may be due to my belief that the most important things in life cannot be bought, or may be because I've never lived in impoverished circumstances.

How is it then possible for me to achieve all the sales goals that my superiors set for me? "Why are your sales figures so good?" was one of the first questions that my future Great Teacher asked me.

"There are two things that have driven me since I can remember. I'm not a sales person; I'm just a patients' rights activist. I believe each person deserves the best possible treatment, even an elderly lady in a remote little village. I believe my work helps others. I love my clients and they love me," I replied.

To me, doctors are not potential prescriptors of our medications; they are people, who, I'm sure, do their best to help their patients. What's being sold is emotions, and emotional intelligence plays a key role.

When I visit my doctors, I don't think about how many boxes of medication I will sell. I only think about whether the doctor will think of patients for whom our medicine could help. Since I strongly

41

believe in "our" medication and in the fact that doctors only want to heal patients, I also believe I work for a good cause.

When a nurse who's been using our medication tells me, "You know what? A patient who could not even walk to a grocery store climbed Triglav (the highest mountain in Slovenia) this summer," I'm really proud.

And in all these years, there have been many such stories told about patients.

Who would you buy a bicycle from?

Would it be with someone who explains to you the fervor of all the things you'll be able to do if you buy the bicycle, where you'll be able to ride, and how great it'll be—someone whose passion can be heard in their voice?

Or, would you prefer to buy it from a dim salesperson, who's only explaining to you the technical properties of the bicycle?

Of course, some highly rational people (usually men) will be interested in only the technical properties.

Always lend a sympathetic ear to a fellow human so that, in the shortest time possible, you can recognize what they're interested in or what problem they have—and offer them a solution.

We ask too little. If you want to know something or if you're confused, ask. Be straightforward and upfront. You may not get an answer, but at least you've tried.

We are often misled by assumptions.

WE ARE ALL JUST PEOPLE

"Behind the mask of ice that people wear, there beats a heart of fire."

- Paulo Coelho

The manager who hired me, who's a doctor herself, gifted me the following teaching before I commenced work, "Doctors are just people, like you. They're not gods. You'd be surprised to see how many of them are really unhappy and insecure. Never forget that you're as very well educated and paid as they are. You're working for a good cause, too."

Of course, she had told me all this with a purpose. She knew all too well where she was sending me and what I was up against, and I wouldn't have guessed it in my wildest dreams.

I've met many influential, awe-inspiring people. I've had the opportunity to interact with many executive managers, scientists, to hosting leading-edge, world-renowned experts in various fields of medicine.

Oh, how I was afraid of utter nonsense. We've been raised to fear authority and those who are "important." Is it our own insecurities that make us think of other people as super humans? I've learned that behind all those titles there are but ordinary people. Very often they are lovely and not haughty at all. They openly discuss their families, work, and hobbies.

After doing fieldwork for a while, I started feeling bored, and the only challenge were the so-called "difficult and unapproachable doctors."

Why does being persistent pay off?

EXAMPLE NO. 1:

When I first paid him a visit, he refused to shake my hand. The way he looked at me was anything but kind.

"What do you want?" He asked me curtly. As he was head of the department, I had to ask him for permission to attend a morning doctors' meeting and present the novelties. For quite a while, no one from our company had visited these doctors, and I found it imperative that our medicine be present there as well.

Why had no one been visiting them? I wondered. Reluctantly, he ordered an exact meeting time. I came to his office again, and offered to shake his hand, which he also refused. The same happened a few more times. During meetings, he would ask difficult questions; in other words, he wasn't hospitable and kind. But I persisted.

One day, when I was sick and tired of his indifferent attitude, I gathered my courage and asked him what the problem really was. He explained that he had been holding an old grudge against our company and that he didn't like us. That was when he took the time to talk with me. It was a crucial moment in our relationship, and ever since that day, it's been him who's supported me in all collective projects and who's been delighted in receiving my visit.

EXAMPLE NO. 2:

A family doctor. His waiting room was always packed. He took all the time needed for his patients. Everyone praised how good a doctor he was. Each time I visited him, he smiled, greeted me, offered me a seat, and listened to me. He never talked. He never asked a question. I just kept visiting his office regularly, said what I needed to say, thanked him, and left. I never pushed him, because I was under the impression that he didn't like being pushed. I never asked him anything. After a while, I learned that this doctor, in treating a specific illness, used our medicine most frequently.

Experience has taught me to see a human in every person, to release my fears, and ask myself what I want to achieve.

I've read about Slovenian doctors, namely the most threatened group are women—family doctors between the ages of 41 and 50—who die younger than the same age groups in other professions. Research has also shown an increased level of stress among young doctors. The causes are the high level of responsibility, serious and time-limited decision-making, overworking under a severe psychological burden, the constant dissatisfaction of people, an increasing number of administrative tasks, and a reduced influence on decision-making about work processes. For young female doctors, working in emergency rooms is especially stressful, as they are held doubly responsible for their jobs and their families. This kind of lifestyle consequentially ends in a high rate of suicides, drug abuse, and depression.

Remember: we are all just people. We mercilessly expect these doctors to make flawless decisions, and allow them no room for mistakes.

Also, when I spoke with doctors about what they appreciated most in the pharmaceutical company representatives who visited them, they prioritized kindness, unobtrusiveness, expertise, professional conduct, time flexibility, and taking into account their suggestions and remarks. They dislike obtrusive, aggressive, and lengthy visits.

One day, a dear Teacher of mine wrote, "A river cuts through a rock not with its power, but with persistence."

Persist.

A GREAT TEACHER

"Come to the edge," he said.
They said, "We are afraid."
"Come to the edge," he said. They came. He pushed
them and they flew.

- Guillaume Apollinaire

I don't know her particularly well, but in my eyes, she has always been one of those rare people who do their job with the utmost joy and have found their life's purpose. On this day, we met to discuss a collective project we had been working on. After we'd finished work for the day, we order coffee at a hospital bar. She began talking about the new management at work, and I could see a deep disappointment in her eyes. She could hardly hold back the tears.

She explained how her new superior had no experience within that field, how they were humiliating people, doing people injustice, and trampling them. I listened to her, then advised her.

Throughout my career, many different superiors had been changed; I was close to despair, but there was only one solution.

You have to change the way you see people. They will never change themselves.

Find a reason for why your superiors act a certain way. They are often very unhappy and carry wounds from their childhood. For example, living with demanding parents whom they want to prove themselves to, yet still, their parents are dissatisfied with what they have achieved. Perhaps they wish to prove themselves to their partner or they can't show their worth to their family, or are simply disregarded and trampled upon at home, which, consequently, makes them use their position of power at work. Have compassion for them—remind yourself of how very happy you can be, because you, I hope, don't have such problems.

Your only job is to change your opinion of these people and begin to think about them with compassion. Personally, I try to find in everyone—even in those people I like the least—one positive quality or skill, and learn it from them.

It's been a long time since I last perceived my superiors as people who fume all the time and stack more and more work upon me. I now see them as my Great Teachers. Once we master a lesson in our relationships, some of them/us will leave and new people will come along.

If you feel you can't do this, it's better to leave before you destroy your health and break your family apart.

After all, we're all replaceable.

MY GREAT TEACHERS

An especially Great Teacher at the beginning of my path

Recently, after many years, he held a lecture for our company again. He hasn't changed at all; he still gives the same performance and holds the same beliefs. Most of the attendees haven't met him yet. Some of us, however, he's left a deep mark. He used to be my colleague at my university faculty, and as early as then, he was clearly special. When I began my job, he was an expert colleague doing fieldwork. He did this for two years, and after only a month after my arrival, he was promoted. A new position was created that hadn't existed before—head of expert associates. Suddenly, we were no longer school friends or equal associates. He became my Teacher.

Since I was new, he did his best and resolved to teach me all the sales skills I needed. He didn't just want me to be an excellent sales person, he wanted me to be an outstanding one. Each week, he would join me at least once in visiting the doctors. He showed me how to knock on their door, how to ask questions and listen to what a doctor was saying, how to organize my work, and how to take notes and plan. We did, in fact, argue here and there, when we shared different views. But the knowledge he imparted generously on me still benefits me, and I remember his directions more often than not.

Later, he became a sales skills coach for the entire region. He was a man who really loved our company and made us feel like he would never leave. Today, he has his own company, he holds lectures occasionally, and is making a living out of his favorite hobby.

My dear school friend, after all these years, I am still grateful for your patience and devotion in helping me.

If you want to have real teachers, know that in pharmacy, many are willing to share their expertise and experience.

A really Great Teacher

We were all eagerly awaiting her arrival. We were told she was the "dread" of the pharmaceutical industry. Most of the people spoke ill of her, and we felt uneasy about our uncertain future. Would we meet her high expectations?

She entered the room. Smiling. Elegant. Gracious. Kind. Intelligent. I was fortunate without being aware that she would become my Teacher. She was somebody who kept reiterating that nothing was impossible, and mercilessly pushed me out of my comfort zone. She demanded more and more; she wanted me to be different, sharp, aggressive, and as ambitious as she was herself. And gorgeous. What took me by surprise was that she wasn't envious— she wanted her closest associates to be elegant, too. She would never hide that she used to be dissatisfied with her looks. But she made it and has earned who she is today. Many colleagues were inspired by her to awaken their femininity within, including myself.

She always has and always will do everything for her team to be the best. She understands she's successful when her team is successful. And never will she let her team down. She will always stand right by their side. That's another reason why it felt good to be part of her team.

It took me a long time to be able to write about her like this. It used to hurt me to not believe her loud "Good morning!" as she stepped into the office with a smile on her face. It wasn't a real smile and I could feel that. When one day I had had enough, I asked her why she wore that fake smile every day.

She looked at me and replied, "I don't want a single soul to find out how really bad I feel. People would rejoice to know I'm not well." After she had acknowledged that, I finally let her into my heart.

I no longer saw an enemy in her. Instead, I saw a person who was sent into my life to remind me what I ought to do myself in order to see people in a good light.

Today, I'm deeply grateful to her as she has taught me many invaluable things. I experience her as a person—who feels uniquely—and helping others is in her best interest.

She can judge people very well and always steer them in the right direction.

I have often shared with her, "You'd be a perfect First Lady."

A male Great Teacher

Energies flow differently when a man leads a team. He was my Teacher only for a brief period, but he infused my thinking with a man's rationality and sobriety; in other words, he took a very male approach to certain things. He explained the world of numbers to me and gave me a hard time with tables and analyses, which I dislike. I've learned, however, to scan and read numbers, too. He knew how to commend people and openly stated when he disagreed. Clearly, he saw things from a male perspective. Things always had to be rational, and rationality itself is benefical every so often.

Among other things, I see the father in him. As he talks about his children, he oozes love. He loves to travel, just like I do, so we never run out of topics to discuss. Thank you.

A Teacher with a heart of gold

Upon her arrival, I understood how it felt to have someone who appreciated and trusted me, who encouraged and supported me by my side. She's sharp, hard-working, and persistent. A woman of action, she never waits; she does everything right away. I admire her. As she has abundant experience from working in various pharmaceutical companies and positions, she can judge accurately what the people on her team need. She understands that we're all different, and she appreciates the work of every individual. She knows that every so often one needs to stop, have a coffee, and chat in peace.

She brings into her team the people she deems emotionally mature and enthusiastic. She doesn't appreciate laziness. You can talk about anything with her, or entrust her with your problems, which she will never give away. She always lends a helping hand. She adores books and lends them generously. She understands we all have our private lives—with our ups and downs. She creates a work atmosphere where you're thrilled to be back at work.

To her, a good leader is someone who sets people free; who trusts them completely and gives them free reign.

And freedom is that which brings about new ideas and promotes satisfaction at work.

I like being part of her team.

I'm infinitely grateful to you, my Teacher with a heart of gold.

An important Great Teacher

What to do when the boss of bosses announces that they will join you in the field? When one December day this happened to me, I was so tired with all the projects I was finalizing that it was all the same to me.

"Of course, let him come with me," I said. How was I to be composed throughout the day and drive both of us safely back to the company? I resolved to be completely honest with him about everything: what I was doing, what I had done, and what the problems were. He's been on many double visits. He's an excellent psychologist. He saw how enthusiastic I was about doing my job. I took him along to all of my most important doctors. He untied his tie and spoke with them. I was astounded with how well-rounded his medical expertise was. We spent a great day together and I was delighted that he got to know my work and me. When he looks at my numbers, he knows who's behind them.

Use the situations you fear to your advantage.

Yes, even bosses are only people.

Real Teachers love to see you as audacious, different, and risk taking. They see mistakes as lessons from which you have learned something.

This is what I want to shout from the rooftops: Change the way you look at people, and your world will change for the better.

**Be grateful for all the people who push
you out of your comfort zone and make
you see everything through fresh eyes.
Limitations only exist in the mind.**

How do Great Teachers think?

1. Everything is possible.
2. They want to hear solutions; they aren't interested in problems.
3. The only constant in life is change.

COLLEAGUES AND INNER SELF-PROMOTION

"The relationships we have with the world are largely determined by relationships we have with ourselves."

- Greg Andersen

A really Great Teacher was sure that your colleagues will know nothing of what you do or how successful you are at what you do unless you show it, and so she introduced a so-called self-promotion within the company.

"You know, you have to work with your colleagues just like with the doctors. If you treat them as you treat the doctors, they'll all help you out faster," she advised me.

I agreed with that, but I usually had little time for my colleagues. When in my office, I would take care of administrative things in the shortest time possible. Sometimes, I had no time to chat. She was right.

Self-praise is something most of us normally avoid. We think others will notice the things we've done and how good we've been. As it turns out, most people don't notice this. If you'd ever exposed yourself and shared what you'd done, they'd suddenly see you differently. Clearly, we were all quite embarrassed when one of us had to expose themselves, but it surely stuck in my colleagues' minds. And now, they all know what we've done and how successful we are.

Another crucial thing is that we work together. Those who are involved in our projects are told how important their contribution is.

If you ever want to get a second opinion about something, let your colleagues from other departments help you with it.

Perhaps you're looking for fresh ideas or a reconstruction. If so, call people to a "brainstorming session" and ask those who know little about your field of work and who aren't burdened with it what they think.

They'll find original solutions and point out potential misassumptions. Thus, you'll also make new alliances in relationships.

TO MOTIVATE THE EMPLOYEES OR NOT?

"Just one small positive thought in the morning can change your whole day."

- Dalai Lama

We often talk about how to motivate employees so they can become more enthusiastic about what they do. Is it a company's job to motivate individual employees or the job of each individual to motivate themselves?

I approve of companies striving to create working conditions that attract the most qualified job seekers, and a working environment that offers a sense of safety in sharing opinions openly, without facing negative repercussions.

It's my wish that those who apply for a job apply for it because they believe they'll be able to grow and learn from it—and also because they believe in the company of their choice and its vision.

There are many people who take up jobs that mean diddly squat to them; who only keep coming to work because of the salary or the reward they'll get if they exceed expectations.

If I employed people, I'd employ those that don't have to be additionally motivated and can recognize the advantages and value of their working environment themselves.

Even after so many years of doing what I do, I still pinch myself when I see in front of me the inscription of my company or hear on the television news about the medicine we're successfully developing.

That's when I remind myself, "Yes, you work for a publicly renowned and successful company. You can be proud."

We're not proud enough and loyal enough to our places of employment; we should kick our passion up a few notches.

We're all fundamentally different. Some people would do anything for a promised trip, a better car, some extra money, or a promotion to a different position.

Then there's a group of people who are satisfied with a lower monthly salary and a permanent job that gives them a sense of security.

And there are other people who are motivated by sheer praise.

Appreciate those who give you your "daily bread."

OR GO HOME AND GET ANOTHER JOB

"There is nothing either good or bad, but thinking makes it so."

- William Shakespeare

I've never lost a job, but I've witnessed quite a few stories where loss ended up leading to a dream come true.

About twenty years ago, a friend shared with me how eager he was to work in a world-renowned educational institution some day. Back then, he had already been following all the research and work that went on at such institutions. Two years ago, I received a letter from him saying that he had lost his job that he really loved as well as his family, and that he had no future plans whatsoever. He had just turned fifty. There was nothing that could cheer him up and he was fighting depression. His job meant the world to him.

After years of working abroad, he resolved to return home for a year. In less than a year, he got married, found his long-searched for love, and told me that he was overjoyed as he had—finally—also got the job at the institution he had dreamt about twenty years ago.

Today, he's the luckiest man in the world. He's got it all. Without losing his job and hitting rock bottom, he would have never found true happiness.

An acquaintance had successfully concluded a cumbersome project at work, went on an eagerly-awaited vacation with her three little children, and when she first got back to work, they told her they no longer needed her. She was taken aback as she had not expected this after many successful projects. Today, less than a year after she was sacked, she's working from home and doing things that used to be an expensive hobby of hers, and for which she hardly found time. She's now independent and is always there for her little children, while she used to be away from home more often than not. She dared to follow her heart.

After giving birth to a child, a friend of mine started her own business. Due to many debtors, her company was operating in the red. Just as she and her partner had moved into a new house, he lost his job. As their finances spiraled downwards, the discord between them grew.

In the end, they split up, and sold the company and the house. We were sitting together when she was daydreaming of a partner who would really love her and of how her financial problems would some day disappear. Before long, she found a new partner and they had a baby. He's a very caring father and his company is thriving. Does she live the way she imagined she would at her lowest moments? Is she happy?

She would simply respond, "Very!"

A dear friend of mine called me a few days ago. She was made redundant in a company where she had spent fifteen years working from morning till night. She could feel something coming for quite some time.

My only comment was, "Great! You'll be able to live your passion. Open a pastry shop!"

Always know that each thing that looks horrible at first contains the path to your dreams.

It may sound "crazy," but we should be thankful for new opportunities and appreciate those who've laid our path to these opportunities by creating adversity.

We always set limits on ourselves, but we ought to always dream "big."

REWARD FOR A JOB WELL DONE

"The highest reward for a person's toil is not what
they get for it, but what they become by it."
- John Ruskin

What do you expect in return for a job well done? Are you happy with only your salary? Do you expect a bonus payment, a paid vacation, a better position, praise, or the *Employee of the Year* title?

I've received all that. And it used to mean a lot to me. However, I now see a reward for a job well done from a completely different vantage point.

EAACI Congress; Austria: Vienna
June 2016

I've been spending these days in Vienna, as my job enabled me to be one of the attendees of the European Congress of Allergy and Clinical Immunology.

On the first day of the Congress I rushed to a lecture at the Congress center, I met a world-renowned expert in the field of medicine I'm currently working in. He was hosted in Slovenia at the beginning of this year. What an incredibly beautiful feeling it was to see a man of this grandeur happy to see you. Plus, it's great to know people like him, since good doctors are often what patients need most.

Having the privilege of attending lectures and having access to information on the latest diagnostic and therapeutic possibilities is, to my mind, it's an immense added value to my work.

Working at an international company offers countless opportunities for personal as well as professional growth.

You get to learn how to respond fast, and to think and adjust differently.

There are many chances for promotion.

I attended a meeting where I interacted with colleagues from Brazil, Finland, Denmark, Canada, India, and elsewhere. We shared our experiences and examples of good practice. We spoke about problems and had opportunities to innovate. I appreciate it when those who drive the global strategy for a particular medicine want to know what we think and are receptive to our ideas. After a meeting, my colleagues and I walked a bit around the city. I've known some of them for a while; we've been emailing each other and always look forward to meeting again.

Tomorrow has new meetings in store for me—new acquaintances, new knowledge, and a short ramble around the city.

A teacher has told me to have a "punch cake" at Sacher Hotel. And writing my book at night awaits.

Yes, life is beautiful!

What means a lot to me? The opinion of my colleagues.

When a colleague of mine was leaving for another job, her words deeply moved me.

She said, "I'll think of you a lot in my new job. I've really appreciated your way of doing things and your thinking. I'd like to be more like you in this regard."

Could one ask for more?

Or there was this other colleague of mine, who, after we'd looked at the sales numbers the day before, said during lunchtime, "I was thinking about you at night. You always show excellent results. You're never pushy or aggressive. You should teach us how to be like that."

Sitting at the same table was another colleague, who added, "I think about you a lot, too. You never expose yourself. Still, you do an excellent job."

There was a seminar a few days ago held by a British expert. She holds seminars all over the world, each week in a different place, and she's published many professional books. Her son is the same age as mine, eleven. The conversation turned to my family's travels and my book. She must have sensed my great enthusiasm about everything that was said, and told me I was her inspiration. She decided to travel with her son to Africa the following year and volunteer there.

That's how I got the confirmation I needed that writing a book was the right decision.

I derive my greatest pleasure from meeting a client of mine after many years who's still happy to see me—and I'm happy to see them.

Who I am, who I can potentially become, and who I'm becoming is the greatest reward for my work.

All that I've written in this chapter called *Do what you love* can be used anywhere—in anything you do, in your private life as well.

Do all that you do with all your heart.

CHAPTER THREE

OUR WELL-BEING

"There are moments when troubles enter our lives and we can do nothing to avoid them.

"But they are there for a reason. Only when we have overcome them will we understand why they were there."

- Paulo Coelho

IT'S ABOUT THEM

"It is health that is real wealth and not pieces of gold or silver."

- Mahatma Gandhi

She

Looking at her sweet face, I see her eyes sparkling here and there, just like the day we met. Her spirited laughter used to reverberate all around. She would laugh a lot, liked having fun, and had many friends. When an illness crept into her life, she was at the peak of her creativity. She took her job seriously, constantly overworked herself, and tried to please everybody. When after a diagnosis, her doctor advised her against having a baby, she never returned to that doctor again.

"What should I live for, then?" she wondered at the age of thirty. During her pregnancy, she was brimming with energy. She gave birth to her son, but her health deteriorated further with each passing month. It took her a long time to admit that her strength was waning, but there came a day when she could no longer manage and she ended up in a wheelchair. Today, she's completely dependent on the help of others. Her arms and legs don't serve her anymore. Her son is growing.

Each time she goes to rehabilitation, he gifts her with a drawing he did when he was little. It is a drawing of a wheelchair thrown in the garbage and of his mommy walking. When someone suffers this heavy illness, they often lose their partner and friends. Most of her friends have gone. Those who've stayed are her real friends and her family. She spends most of her days alone, reading books, crying, and dreaming. There are days when she'd rather just be gone, but her love for her son gives her strength. We're sitting on her balcony and her gaze fixates on a cherry tree. It's been four years since she last picked those cherries.

"You know," she tells me hopefully, "there will come the day, when I'll be able to pick those cherries myself."

When she celebrated her thirtieth birthday, she was told her diagnosis—multiple sclerosis. Multiple sclerosis is still an incurable disease.

Multiple Sclerosis (MS)

Multiple sclerosis is the most common debilitating illness among young adults between the ages of 20 and 40. According to the estimate of the Slovenian MS Association, there are more than 3500 people with MS in Slovenia. More women than men fall ill, with women making up 2/3 of cases. An MS diagnosis is rarely given to people younger than 12 and older than 55. The medicine that could cure it hasn't been discovered yet, and the same is true of the cause of the disease. It's an autoimmune disease of the central nervous system that affects the protective cell membrane (myelin cell membrane) of a nervous cell. Due to this damage, information isn't successfully communicated through the nerves, which most frequently manifests in:

- Impairment of vision
- Impairment of hearing
- Loss of balance

- Lower and upper limb defects
- Fatigue
- Cognitive thinking problems
- Urinary incontinence.

Most patients experience MS in terms of consecutive deterioration and improvement. Some people experience MS in a progressive form. What's worst is the unpredictability of the disease, as it is not known when a certain form of deterioration may occur.

She's my inspiration. Because of her, I appreciate life all the more.

He

Rests. Doesn't talk much. His mother talks... about what he may or may not do. When she's with him, she tries to be strong, but sometimes she cannot hold back her tears before him. She helps him.

Most of the nights she cries and wonders, "Why him?" What did they do wrong, what did she do wrong? What should she have done?

He's gone through his tenth chemotherapy, the strongest so far. He feels sick, his body keeps weakening, and this is only the beginning of a long treatment. There's a whole year of chemotherapy and a difficult operation ahead of him. His hair has fallen out and his face is covered in pimples. When he fell three months ago while skiing, he thought his leg was still hurting due to the fall. Then he noticed a small lump. He was taken to the doctors. When after the medical check-up a nurse held his mother compassionately, his mother knew instantly that something was terribly wrong. They had given him a diagnosis right away: osteosarcoma.

Osteosarcoma

Osteosarcoma is the second most frequent primary bone cancer tumor. It is most frequent with patients between the ages of 10 and 20, and it can occur at any age. Sometimes it occurs with elderly patients with Paget's disease. Around half of these tumors appear close to the knee, and they can develop in any bone. They can spread into the lungs and cause pain and swelling. In order for it to be diagnosed, a biopsy needs to be done first. It's treated with a combination of chemotherapy and operations.

He's only 15 years old. The disease mercilessly broke into his youth and changed the course of his life plans.

"What would you like to do when it's all over?" His mother asked him.

"I'd like to play football again," he answered.

It's going to be a tough and long fight, but he's a fighter alright.

Because of him, I'm deeply grateful for the health of my children.

These two stories are only two among many, but they've left a powerful mark upon my life.

There are people who fight for their lives and the lives of their loved ones every day.

When an illness creeps into someone's life, one begins to see their own lives in a completely new way. Small things, like an untidy apartment, little money, bad school grades, and ornery bosses no longer matter.

An Australian nurse named Bronnie Ware used to work for many years in palliative care with people who only had 3 to 12 weeks to live. Based on her experience and her developing close relationships with them, she wrote a book called *The Top Five Regrets of the Dying.*

The top five wishes of the dying are:

1. I wish I'd had the courage to live a life true to myself, not the life others expected of me.
2. I wish I hadn't worked so hard.
3. I wish I'd had the courage to express my feelings.
4. I wish I had stayed in touch with my friends.
5. I wish that I had let myself be happier.

Most of the people on their deathbed don't wish they had won the lottery or earned more money, says Bronnie Ware.

I'm sure all these people would give anything for a cure that would prolong their life.

What about you?

Researchers look for new cures every day, and pharmaceutical companies invest billions of dollars in the development of new medicines.

The cost of developing a new cure is around two billion dollars, and it takes ten to fifteen years before scientists discover the most effective compound among thousands of compounds and then register it. That's the last part of the process, which is only achieved by less than 15 percent of all research.

As part of the clinical research of new cures, patients are given new chances. Often times they recover or their lives are prolonged.

Do you ever ask yourself how much a life is worth? And what you would give for it?

All our problems are nothing compared to our desire to live, but not being able to or sitting powerlessly and waiting for what's going to happen, or wanting so much to create and to experience life.

We, who are healthy, have all the chances for a full life. Usually, it is us alone who create obstacles and complicate simple things. Life is simple. We simply live it in accordance with what we feel. Let's be who we are and let's shine all our light.

When you really want to do something with all your heart and experience fear, remember of all the sick people and be at least as brave as they are.

Do it. For yourself and for all the people you love who cannot do it themselves.

Be just as brave as the people,
who fight every day for themselves or for their close relatives.

WE MATTER MOST

"Don't wait until something special happens, begin sooner.

"Think little, do some good, eat some 'healthy' food, and above all—try to be a better person each day.

"This ought to be the guiding lines for all, who got their ticket to appear in their physical form on planet Earth. Let's use this ticket wisely and make this world a better place."

— *Alen Kobilica*

After he'd called a meeting of all the employees and I noticed champagne and cake, I first thought he was leaving. But he wasn't. As we held our glasses up, he emphasized, "We are the ones that matter most."

Do I hear it right? He's putting words on my paper. He said we were working well and achieving great results.

"If you spoke more to one another, approached colleagues of yours and talked with them, you'd avoid many misunderstandings," he advised.

Still, what matters most is for us to remain healthy and happy.

Many people drive themselves too hard and work all the time.

As weariness grows, dissatisfaction within families does, too. Marriages fall apart, children get into trouble, and someone ends up with health problems. Everything can fall apart in an instant.

We take life too seriously. We forget to be happy, and above all, to be ourselves.

Is it wrong to pass idle time every now and then, and do absolutely nothing?

When, about a year after I had taken up a new challenge and worked all day and night, I was driving home one evening—so mentally exhausted that I didn't care at all if I crashed or not—I knew I had hit bottom. It seemed like I was on the edge of a cliff and only a single jump could take me to peace. I saw no one, I heard no one. I arrived home and hugged my kids.

I understood I had to get myself out of this state of mind as soon as possible. A few days later, we packed our suitcases and went skiing. We skied in complete wilderness; there was not a soul anywhere, one could only hear the wind howling. I went sound asleep for two days. During the day, I skied and gasped for silent air.

Then, I unwrapped the present my brother had given me for my birthday. It was the book *The Magic* by Rhonda Byrne. After I'd read it, I felt as if a stream of pure water had travelled through my body and washed away all the bad feelings and thoughts. A week of solitude with my family saved my life.

I can affirm that I've changed—my view of work, of myself, and of life.

There's hardly a thing that takes me off my path nowadays—and it's been three years since then. I'm well aware of what I have and how important it is to add less seriousness to life.

On behalf of all the sick, we, who have everything and yet complain incessantly, should live a full life.

Have I changed anything in particular, apart from not sweating the small stuff anymore?

An anaesthetist my age stood by me and read a statement that I needed to fill in and sign before a surgical procedure.

"Ma'am, would you like to be driven here by an ambulance next time? When did you last have a preventive medical check-up?"

Her voice sounded dreadfully serious, and I was beside myself due to the state I was in. I so wanted to "come to my senses" before an illness caught up with me.

I didn't reply, she waited for a few moments, then said, "Why am I even telling you this? I work non-stop myself."

Perhaps that event shook me enough to finally do something for myself.

Say thanks every day for all that you are given and for each day you get to live. Whether it's good or bad, everything leaves a mark on us and makes us stronger and wiser.

> *"If the only prayer you ever say in your entire life*
> *is thank you, it will be enough."*
>
> *- Meister Eckhart*

CHAPTER FOUR

WE AND A 48-HOUR BREAK

"I got you to look after me, and you got me to look after you, and that's why."

- John Steinbeck

Do you know this scene?

You've finished your work for the day. You're rushing to get your children home from kindergarten or school, taking them to extracurricular activities. Then, in the meantime, you go shopping, are loaded up with shopping bags, your briefcase, your child's cardigan, and what have you, until finally, you arrive home breathing heavily. There are one, two, or three children shouting behind you. Your husband is working or doing his afternoon workout. Your house is a mess, your children are hungry, you are tired and edgy. Since the children won't stop shouting, you're shouting, too. You're cooking in a hurry, tidying, pulling your children apart so that none of them gets hurt during a fight. You keep telling the kids to do their homework, to practice playing this instrument, and do this and that.

Day after day… hurry in the morning—hurry in the evening.

Raised blood pressure in the morning, raised blood pressure in the evening. When your husband comes back, you shout at him, too.

And you ask yourself, "Who (what) have I become? Who am I?"

The women of our generation were raised to be good—to do everything, to try to be perfect.

In a recent interview for *Nedelo,* a Slovenian magazine, Slovenian actress Zvezdana Mlakar said, "I have this quality, where people trust me and feel good in my company. However, I wasn't aware of that. I was a typical Slovenian little girl, who needed to be good, and I didn't know who I really was. For decades, and just like many people, I've tried to please others. I am now less and less good, and more and more authentic."

Regardless of how hard a woman tries, sooner or later she understands that she cannot be a perfect wife, a perfect mother, a perfect housewife, or a perfect employee.

Can she be who she really is?

My younger brother told me the other day, "At your age, couples usually break up, there's a whole lot of them who've broken up and taken up sports—they cycle, run, hike. They explore Slovenia."

What he said did make me laugh, but after a short deliberation, I had to agree.

I recently met an acquaintance whom I haven't seen for months.

"Come, I need to share something with you," she told me cheerfully. "My life has completely changed in the past year. At the beginning of the year, my husband left me. He had fallen in love with another woman. I was desperate, then every other weekend, when he'd look after our kids, I'd go out with my friends. I've met a man. It's amazing, I'm someone's princess again. He treats me so nicely. I've put myself first. I go to the gym twice a week, I've lost weight, and my life is really satisfying."

What's actually a bad experience: the end of the world or a new beginning?

We women often complain about our partners not doing anything for us. They let us change light bulbs by ourselves, carry heavy shopping bags, and when we're sick, we make tea ourselves.

When I recently spoke to a colleague of mine on a business trip, she asked me, "Do you tell him when there's something you can't do? Do you ask him to carry your suitcase because it's too heavy? Do you tell him you feel so sick and that you cannot make tea?"

"No," I replied. "I don't ask him for anything. I take it for granted that he'll notice and do everything." And that only disappointed me; however, I listened to her advice.

When the next day I came home and we were all standing in front of our block of flats, I sighed, "Oh, my suitcase is quite heavy..."

Incredible! Immediately, without saying another word, my husband and my son grabbed my suitcase and carried it for me. It's that easy.

Women, awaken the woman in you!

Say it when there's something you cannot do, and don't try to be a man and a woman at the same time.

Once your man recognizes the feminine gentleness in you, and once you let him be the man, many problems in your relationship will be solved—or they will become solvable again.

And a 48-hour break?

This Friday afternoon, we're going to put our children into care—to grandmas, aunts, and friends—for whom we will return the favour. We only need to pack some of the most important things, sit in the car and drive off. Just me and my darling. We're coming home on Sunday evening, and these are the forty-eight hours that help immensely here and there so that we can remember who we are. An active break or even just sleeping and walking without much planning and rushing so we can feel our flow and heartbeat again. Our children will have a nice time even without us. Let's give our children some breathing space sometimes, so we can breathe ourselves, too.

If only we could do this more often...

It pays to try. Children always want both of their parents to be happy.

CHAPTER FIVE

COOL MOM

"You are what you believe yourself to be."

- Paulo Coelho

When one morning we dropped our children off at school, we happened to meet the parents of five of our children's school friends at a café. We took some time to chat, and the conversation turned to our wishes.

The only father among them said, "A month ago, we sold our house. We let go of a two hundred and fifty square meter house for a sixty square meter rental apartment. We find it really small, but we get around. After many years, I'm loan free again. We're now going to slowly renovate our old house. And there's more! I've changed my job. I want a new challenge..."

A mother among them shared, "My dream is to work in interior design. I've started blogging about it."

"I have to reconsider what else I can offer my clients in my fabric and wool store," said a friend of mine.

Without the fourth person, Andreja, sipping coffee with us,

you'd still not be reading this book today. She eagerly admitted, "I want to publish a book! I'm attending a lecture in Ljubljana next week. Petra Škarja is giving her first lecture entitled *How To Publish A Book.*"

Andreja and I attended the lecture together. Her book *A Book of Life, A Guide Into Your Inner World,* is going to be published, too, in the next days.

How simple it all is, if we just take the time for a chat and reveal our wishes to someone.

And this is how "the idea of moms networking" was born while writing this book.

When you ponder some of the things that didn't happen by chance, more good ideas are born.

With glitter in my eyes, I shared with the headmaster my suggestion about founding a mom's club at the school my children attend. He loved the idea and offered to give me all the help I needed.

In a rush of conviction that that was exactly what the mothers and I needed, I called the first meeting. Want to know how it went? What the response was? Did any mothers attend the meeting at all?

Allow me to proudly share with you the contents of our first meeting.

Dear mothers,

We met yesterday for the first time. We were getting to know each other, revealing our dreams and revelling in the dreams we have already fulfilled. There was much we had to say, as ideas were pouring in, and the meeting just flew by.

Many mothers showed up, and though many hadn't been able to attend, we have received all your good wishes.

What fruits have our socializing born?

1. *The name! Let's call ourselves COOL MOMS.*
2. *We filled out a questionnaire that you will find attached, and that you can fill out if you didn't attend the first meeting. We're going to create a DATA BASE to know who we are, what our skills are, and what we want.*
3. *One of our mothers is going to make our club's logo.*
4. *There will be space at the school's Christmas fair (perhaps elsewhere as well), where every mother under the patronage of COOL MOMS will be able to present her work (on leaflets, business cards, etc.) or sell her products.*
5. *The House of Fruits has kindly offered their seminar rooms should we need them for workshops or other activities as well as their kitchen and a sewing machine. They are also organizing various lectures that we have been kindly invited to attend.*
6. *We've expressed a wish to have potluck dinners with some great music, or even an excursion …*

    • *Would you like to give your wardrobe some fresh air or do you need expert help?*
    • *Have you been trying to lose weight to no avail and dreaming about being in perfect shape?*
    • *Do your children adore stick cake, but you have never managed to make one? Why not let a mom bake it for you?*
    • *Physiotherapy?*
    • *Are you renovating your apartment or house and need an interior designer's advice?*
    • *Are your teenage children having problems with acne or hair? Having problems with cellulite? There's a mom who knows how to help you and will gladly rally round you!*

- *Like sewing or knitting? There are moms that have all the needed materials, and moms who adore doing handiwork. There aren't just a few. There are enough for a business.*☺
- *Why not buy your new phone from an expert whom you can meet in a school corridor every day?*
- *Do you know what so-called handling is and how it can benefit your child?*
- *Yoga, pilates, and more?*
- *Why search for an accountant when there's one in the class?*
- *Would you like to write and publish a book, but you don't know how?*
- *Need to create a good presentation?*
- *Or a larger network of potential clients?*
- *Are you searching for something, but you don't know what that is? Looking for new ideas?*
- *Need help finding a job?*

COOL MOMS ARE HERE FOR ALL THIS AND MORE!
EVERYTHING IS POSSIBLE.
AND TOGETHER WE ARE STRONGER!

We've decided to meet once a month (more often, if necessary) on every first Tuesday.
New ideas and new members are most welcome. ☺

You are cordially invited.
Kind regards!
Lara

Women want to and have to connect and listen to each other and help each other. Rather than being envious, we can exchange our knowledge and rich experiences. There's so much we can learn together and so many new stories of success we can create.

We're now Cool Moms, we have a name that represents the beginning of a new life and a cool name that our children love, too.

What kind of a Cool Mom do children wish to have?

One who is gentle and strong at the same time, one who sticks up for herself and for her child, one who follows her dreams and knows how to encourage a child's dream. Children want a mom who laughs a lot; a mom who has so much energy that she can follow her children's sparks. A mom who understands even when her children are different than she had imagined them to be and even when they do things differently than she would have wanted. They want a mom who also accepts mistakes. A mom who cooks for them and teaches them how to cook. A mom who tells them fairy-tales and later lets her children believe in those fairy-tales. A mom who is patient, amusing, and fun. A mom who is self-confident and brave. A mom who loves—and is loved. A mom who loves to do what she does.

If a mom loves what she does, her children will eagerly want to follow in her footsteps.

Let's be an example to our children!

CONCLUSION

"If one advances confidently in the direction of his dreams, and endeavors to live the life which he has imagined, he will meet with success unexpected in common hours."

- Henry David Thoreau

When I was hired to work at our company, I was sure I'd stay there for two years maximum. In the morning, I'd often leave for fieldwork reluctantly. There were days when I'd feel ill upon entering a hospital... I would stand at the entrance, convincing myself wearily that I had to do my work conscientiously. I felt no passion whatsoever for my job. I only saw problems, and I saw myself as yet another unimportant pharmaceutical company sales representative. My experience was close to none, and I wasn't ready for this kind of work. There's no such university that teaches people how to communicate and the other skills needed for one's job.

People's qualities matter, and so does their flexibility and ability to learn. Quality comes with years of practice in the pharmaceutical industry. Years and years of changes hardened me into a more resilient and, surprisingly, also a more exuberant person. It's only after we hit the bottom that we realize how strong we really are!

The bottom offers a person the chance to change their perspective. Only after we cease complaining can we notice for the first time how many people only complain and are never satisfied with anything. You might have been one of those people yourself, and you may not be able to listen to complainers any more.

Today, I believe in myself and in the work I do, because I know how invaluable I am to so many people's lives. The road I used to travel was full of turns, abysses, stop signs, roundabouts, and crossroads—it caused fear in me—and yet I knew I had to somehow drive through it. It was worthwhile, as this occasionally dangerous road gave birth to my passion, courage, and pride—actually allowing me to become the mother I've always wanted my children to have.

ACKNOWLEDGMENTS

Andrej, you have a wife who loves to dream "big" and has a million crazy ideas. You never doubted me. You always encourage me. You help me. I've chosen the best father for my children.

Luri and Vaal, I couldn't have imagined more perfect children in my wildest dreams. You are my greatest inspiration, my greatest love, and my greatest teachers.

Mom and Dad, I know why I had chosen you. Through you, I've received all the experiences necessary to become who I am today.

Tilen, you've always believed in me. You've always seen me as more beautiful than I've ever seen myself to be. You're the best brother I could ever have.

Dear friends, life without you would be imperfect.

My dear colleagues at work, you understand me and know what I'm talking about. Thank you.

Mr. Školc, thank you very much for your contribution to my daughter's book *I dare. Do you?*

Petra, I don't know if this book would have ever seen the light of day if it hadn't been for you. You've helped many. And you will help many more. Be proud of yourself.

The sleeping little girl has awoken.
Today, she shines in all her beauty.
Her dream has come true.
You're holding her book in your hands.

Thank you very much!

specadeklica@gmail.com

Printed in the United States
by Baker & Taylor Publisher Services